Over 100 games and activities for young people

© Printforce Limited

British Library Cataloguing in Publication Data
A CIP catalogue record for this book is available from the British Library
ISBN 0 948834 08 0

# CONTENTS

## GAMES

*- a collection of noisy, quiet, team and other games to add variety to your programmes.*

## WIDE GAMES

*- a collection for larger numbers of players, played in fields, parks and woodland*

## ICE BREAKERS

*- a collection of games and activities to help get to know one another*

## TREASURE HUNTS

*- a selection of ideas for treasure hunts, designed for minimum leader involvement*

## ACTIVITIES

*- a selection of activities to challenge and inspire young and old*

## INCIDENT HIKE BASES

*- a collection of activities ideal for use as bases in incident hikes or which maybe used as general activities at any time*

## A POCKETFUL OF PROGRAMMES

This book contains a wealth of games and activities for all ages and for a wide range of situations. They have been selected to provide youth leaders with all they need to provide a varied, interesting and challenging programme for their charges at the drop of a hat. Not had time to plan a meeting or session? Then simply dip into this handy book and help will be at hand.

Every activity and game in this book has been thoroughly tried-and-tested by the author and the Members of the 15th Ealing (St. Stephen's) Scout Group and are guaranteed to be great fun! Many thanks to the members and Leaders of the Group, especially to Dave Ludlow, for their inspiration for some of the ideas contained in this collection. Thanks, too, to Emma for editing out some of my poorer ideas.

The book is divided up into sections to allow you to compile your 'instant programme' with ease, accompanied by a rough length of time needed for each game or activity!

Have fun!                           **Dave Wood**

# GAMES

## A collection of noisy, quiet, team and other games to add variety to your programmes.

### STICKY BASKETBALL

EQUIPMENT: a set of 2 'Velcro' catchers and one 'velcro' ball (cheaply available from toy shops or clearance shops)
PLAYERS: ten or more     PLAYING TIME: 15+ mins

• Players divide into two equal teams and stand in their own half of the playing area.

• One player per team is given a 'Velcro'-covered catcher and stands on a chair behind the opposing team.

• The ball is thrown into the playing area and is passed around by the players. No player may run with the ball, no violent tackling permitted. Players must try to get the ball to their team-mate on the chair.

### CHALK NAME RELAY

EQUIPMENT: Sticks of chalk PLAYERS: eight or more
PLAYING TIME: 10+ mins

• Teams sit in relay form. At the other end of the hall, in line with each team, is a square chalked on the floor (use paper and crayons if you can't chalk on the floor).

• Player one in each team has a stick of chalk and, on the word 'GO', runs to the square, chalks his first and last name in the square and runs back, passing the chalk to player two who runs up and writes her name in the square.

• Continue until all have had a turn. Points are awarded for finishing first and for each legible name .

## THE BOTTLE AND THE PEA

EQUIPMENT: drinking straws, dried peas, a milk bottle
& saucer per team
PLAYERS: ten or more    PLAYING TIME: 15+ mins

- Players sit in relay form with a saucer of peas in front of
each team and their milk bottle standing at the far end of the
playing area.
- On the word 'GO', player one from each team grabs a straw
and suck a pea onto its end. She must then run to the milk
bottle with the pea still attached to the end of the straw where
she drops the pea into the bottle.
- After about ten minutes, count up the number of peas in
each bottle to determine the winner.

## FOUR-CORNER BOWL-BALL

EQUIPMENT: 5 washing-up bowls, 8 tennis balls
PLAYERS: 12 or more    PLAYING TIME: 15+ mins

- Players get into four (or three, or five) teams and are
numbered off.
- Teams sit in corners of the playing area with their bowl a
metre in front of them and with the balls in the fifth bowl in
the centre of the playing area.
- The leader calls out a number and the players with that
number run to grab a ball each and back to their bowl into
which they place the ball. If a ball bounces out of the bowl, only
the current player is allowed to put it back in - not her team-
mates.
- The winning team is the first with three balls in its bowl.
- Teams are permitted to take balls from other teams' bowls
to put in their own.

6    *A Pocketful of Programmes*

## ALIEN INVADERS

EQUIPMENT: a plant sprayer
PLAYERS: ten or more    PLAYING TIME: 15+ mins
• Players stand in a circle, with the leader (or Earth Station) in the middle.
• Players are Alien Invaders and stand with their hands by their sides
• The Earth Station fixes the water-filled plant sprayer (brand new and with no traces of chemicals, of course!) to produce a gentle mist and fires it at an invader. The invader 'explodes' unless he raises his deflector shields (ie: a hand held either side of his face like ears).
• The invaders either side of him will explode as well unless they raise the deflector shield closest to the shot invader.
• Exploded invaders sit down and remaining players must be aware as to who is now next to them around the circle.

## HUMAN PINBALL

EQUIPMENT: some chalk
PLAYERS: ten or more    PLAYING TIME: 15+ mins
• Players sit in two equal teams along either side of the hall or playing area and are numbered off (starting at opposite ends as usual).
• Ten or more circles are chalked on the floor between the two teams (use discs of paper or card as an alternative).
• A number is called and the two players with that number stand up, fold their arms and start to hop towards their opponent.
• A player wins if she manages to push her opponent into one of the circles on the floor. A player loses if she puts two feet on the ground or unfolds her arms.

## DARK SQUARE FOOTBALL

EQUIPMENT: a sponge football, a darkened hall
PLAYERS: eight or more   PLAYING TIME: 15+ mins

• Players get into four roughly equal teams and each stand in a separate corner of a hall. Two chalked (or masking tape) lines divide the hall into quarters. The lights are turned off and ball is passed around.

• When the lights are turned on again (after 15 seconds or so), the team in whose quarter the ball happens to be loses a point from a starting total of ten. Points are also lost for any player not in his own quarter when the lights are turned on. The lights are extinguished and play resumes.

• This can be played in daylight with a whistle blown by a blindfolded leader indicating when a point is to be lost.

## ALTERNATE CIRCLE BALL

EQUIPMENT: two footballs
PLAYERS: ten or more   PLAYING TIME: 10+ mins

• Players stand in a wide circle (get them to move out, arms outstretched, until their fingertips touch those of the players either side of them) and they are numbered off

• One ball is given to a player with an ODD number, the other ball is given to a player directly opposite her in the circle who has an EVEN number.

• On the word 'GO', the balls are passed around the circle in a clockwise direction:   ODDS pass only to other ODDS (bypassing the EVENS between them), whilst the EVENS only pass to the next EVEN around the circle.

• The idea is to see if one ball can catch the other one up. If so, the team (ODDS or EVENS) whose ball caught the other one up gains a point.

8

## TUG-O-FOOT

EQUIPMENT: a 2m length of rope, tied to form a loop
PLAYERS: two or more     PLAYING TIME: 15+ mins

• Two players sit facing each other with one leg outstretched, foot pointing directly upwards. The looped rope is put over both players' feet.

• On the word 'GO', players must pull away from each other. The winner is the one who drags her opponent over a marked line. A player loses if the rope slips off her foot.

## LETTER CHANGING

EQUIPMENT: none
PLAYERS: any number     PLAYING TIME: 10+ mins

• Players sit in a circle and somebody chooses a three-lettered word.

• The next player around the circle must change ONE letter in that word to produce a different word. If he can't think of one he loses a point from a starting total of five and the next player takes over.

• Once a new word has been said, it passes on to the next player to, again, change one letter to produce a new word.

• For example, a word such as Joy could become Jot, then Rot, then Rod, Rid, Sid, Sad... and so on.

• If players falter, start again with a new word - or try four letters (but keep 'em clean!).

## DRAGON'S TAIL

EQUIPMENT: a few scarves or hankies etc.
PLAYERS: eight or more PLAYING TIME: 15+ mins

• Players form into two (or more) teams, each with at least four members.

• They form a line in their teams and stand, one behind the other and place their hands on the waist of the player in front of them. The player at the front is the head of the dragon, the player at the back is the dragon's tail and must tuck a scarf or piece of cloth into her belt or waistband to become the dragon's tail.

• On the word 'GO', the head of each dragon must try to grab the tail of the other dragon. If he succeeds then that dragon has won. If a player lets go of the person in front of them, play must pause while they rejoin - penalty points may be added to prevent this happening too frequently.

## WET CUP WANDER

EQUIPMENT: a plastic cup, bowl of water and a measuring jug per team
PLAYERS: eight or more PLAYING TIME: 12+ mins

• Players stand in relay teams with a bowl of water in front of each team and an empty measuring jug at the far end of the (outside) playing area. Each team also has a plastic cup with a number of small holes pierced into its bottom.

• On the word 'GO', player one from each team fills the cup with water and quickly places it on her head, pressing down to minimise water loss! She then runs to the far end where she tips any remaining water.

• After ten minutes or so, the winning team is that which has ferried the most amount of water.

## WINK LEAP

EQUIPMENT: none PLAYERS: 12 or more
PLAYING TIME: 10+ mins

• Half of the players sit in a circle, the other half stand up, one behind each sitting player.

• One sitting player is chosen to be 'It'. She will, at some point, wink directly at another sitting player.

• As soon as a player has been winked at he must leap up and into the centre of the circle.

• The player standing behind him must react quickly and place her hands on his shoulders the second he gets up.

• If the player gets to the middle of the circle, the sitters win a point, if not, the standers win.

• The player who was winked at is now 'It' and the game proceeds.


## LETTER WALKING

EQUIPMENT: none PLAYERS: any number
PLAYING TIME: 5+ mins

• Players line up at one end of the playing area, with the leader at the other.

• The leader calls out a letter of the alphabet and any player with that letter in his or her name may take ONE step forward.

• If their first name contains two of the chosen letter, the player may make two steps.

• Other letters are called out one by one - who reaches the leader first?

## SHOPPING LISTS

EQUIPMENT: Five lists of items (see below)
PLAYERS: any number    PLAYING TIME: 20+ mins

• Five leaders become shopkeepers and stand on chairs around the edge of the room. Each has a problem - one is hard of hearing, one cannot see very well, one whispers, one is a slow thinker and one is forgetful. They each have a list containing items stocked in their shop. Each list is unique.

• The leader running the game stands in the centre of the playing area and gathers the players around her. She asks the players to find the shop which sells (for example) Purple Buttons.

• Players disperse and try to enquire of the shopkeepers (all of whom are overacting) as to who stocks the item.

• Shortly, the correct keeper will identify himself and players must form an orderly queue in front of the shop. The last five players in the queue get a pen mark on their hands as a penalty point.

• Continue for about 8 items. Who has no marks at all?

## NAME DROPPING

EQUIPMENT: a ball (or balloon)
PLAYERS: any number    PLAYING TIME: 15+ mins

• Players stand in a wide circle (fingertips of outstretched arms touching those of their neighbours) with one player in the middle.

• This player throws the ball high in the air, vertically, calling out the name of one of the other players.

• This person must catch the ball before it hits the ground. If she catches it the original player stays in the middle and throws again, if she drops it, she has a turn at throwing.

*A Pocketful of Programmes*

## TAIL CHASING

EQUIPMENT: short lengths of cloth or scarves
PLAYERS: any number      PLAYING TIME: 10+ mins

• Players each have a scarf tucked into the back of their trousers or belts and a wide playing area is defined.

• On the word 'GO', players must try to grab the tails of as many other players as possible - the player with the most tails at the end is the winner. Once a player has lost his tail he must move to the side and may not take any other tails.

## FOUR-GOAL SOCCER

EQUIPMENT: a football (or two)
PLAYERS: 16 or more      PLAYING TIME: 20+ mins

• Four goals are set up in the centre of the sides of a large square pitch.

• Rules are as for normal soccer except that for every goal a goalkeeper lets in, his team gets a penalty point. The team with the least penalty points wins.

• To speed the game up, especially if playing with 30 or more players, use two footballs. A leader may be needed by each goal to record the number of goals let in.

## STICKER SPOTTERS

EQUIPMENT: sticky labels (see below)
PLAYERS: any number      PLAYING TIME: 20+ mins

• Write the name of knots, bandages, physical exercises etc onto sticky labels which you hide around the playing area.

• Players have three minutes to collect as many of these as possible, scoring one point for their teams for each one. They then complete the activity on the stickers they found to score additional points (dependent on the activity).

# CHUBBY BUNNIES

EQUIPMENT: lots of marshmallows
PLAYERS: 2-6 per circle    PLAYING TIME: 8+ mins
- This is a fast-moving game and may be a bit messy!
- Players sit in a circle, with a bowl full of marshmallows in the middle.
- On the word 'GO', player one stuffs a marshmallow into his mouth says 'Chubby Bunnies'- player two does the same and so on around the circle.  Players are NOT allowed to chew or swallow their marshmallows.
- Player one, picks up a second marshmallow, again, says 'Chubby Bunnies'. Continue around the circle as many times as possible.
- A player is out if the words 'Chubby Bunnies' are inaudible, or if he giggles too much or dribbles all over the table!

# HUNT THE CARD

EQUIPMENT: a pack of playing cards
PLAYERS: eight or more   PLAYING TIME: 12+ mins
- Players sit in a large circle, in the middle of which are placed the cards, spread out and lying face-down.
- Three players are chosen and a playing card is called out by the leader.
- The threet dash to the middle, locate the chosen card. using only one hand - the other must be held behind their back and they must turn each card face-down again if it is not the chosen card.
- When a player finds the right card, she must run out of the circle without getting tagged by one of the other card-hunters. If she succeeds she gains a point, if she is tagged, the person tagging her wins the point.
- Repeat with new players and another card.

14

# CROSS THE BRIDGE

EQUIPMENT: chalk

PLAYERS: eight or more    PLAYING TIME: 15+ mins

- A bridge is chalked on the floor (use masking tape as an alternative) measuring about two metres wide, expanding to three metres wide around a blindfolded player who stands at the centre of the bridge (the bridge is now long, thin and with a bulge in the middle).

- Players start at one end of the bridge and must attempt to creep up to, and past, the guardian of the bridge, who is armed with a pillow.

- Players who get walloped have failed in their quest and must go back to try later. Successful players can give guidance to the others.

# INDY 500 BALLOON RACE

EQUIPMENT: a drinking straw and balloon per team, plus a ball of string and some adhesive tape.

PLAYERS: eight or more    PLAYING TIME: 20+ mins

- To begin, a piece of string is stretched from one end of the playing area to the other (between two chairs or sticks), onto which is first threaded half a drinking straw. A balloon is inflated, sealed, and taped to the straw.

- Players sit in relay form at one end of their piece of string, with player one in each team standing by their team's balloon.

- On the word 'GO', player one blows her balloon along the string until it reaches the other end. She then returns to tag player two who runs up and blows the balloon back to the team. Player three blows it to the far end and so on, until the time limit is up (how many trips did it make?) or until, say, 12 journeys have been made.

# PIG

EQUIPMENT: a pack of playing cards
PLAYERS: three to 13     PLAYING TIME: 15+ mins

• Sort out the cards so that there is a set of four matching cards for each player. Shuffle these up and deal four cards to each player in the circle, face down.

• On the word 'GO', each player looks at his cards and, at the same time as the other players, passes one card on to his LEFT. This should be done quickly, so it may be an idea to count 'One, two, three, PASS' each time.

• As soon as a player has four matching cards he puts a finger on his nose. Other players must keep an eye out for anyone doing this and, if they see someone doing it, must copy them. The last player to notice and put his finger on his nose loses that round.

# FRUIT STORY RELAY

EQUIPMENT: a simple story
PLAYERS: eight or more   PLAYING TIME: 12+ mins

• Players sit in relay form and, instead of numbers, are given the names of certain items of fruit. For example, player one in each team would be Apple, player two - Pear... etc.

• The leader tells a simple story which will contain repeated mentions of each of the fruit.

• When a type of fruit is mentioned, the players with that name must stand up, run to the far end of the playing area and back again - first one back in a straight team wins a point.

• When the words 'Fruit Basket' are mentioned, all players must run up and back to their places.

• Vary this with names of dinosaurs, modes of transport... or whatever.

# WIDE GAMES

## A collection of games for larger numbers of players, played in fields, parks and woodland

---

### JOKERS WILD

---

EQUIPMENT: a pack of playing cards, some paper and pens
TIME NEEDED: 20+ mins

• Players are given one playing card each and disperse over the playing area (note: the four Aces and two Jokers must be distributed if playing with less than 52 people).

• Ten other players (including leaders) then set off and try to catch card-holding players. When tagged, players must show their card. The leader adds the face value of the card to the total of others he has caught. Jacks, Queens and Kings count as 11, 12 and 13 respectively. Aces count as 20.

• If a player holding a Joker is caught, the leader's total score is reduced to zero and the holder of the Joker 'keeps' the leader's old score.

• Players are allowed to swap cards around but are only permitted to have one card at a time. This means that leaders will have to be careful who they tag in order to avoid Jokers!

• At the end of the game, the combined scores collected by the two Jokers is compared to the combined totals of all of the leaders - the highest score wins and losers get to do the washing up!

## LIGHT DEFENDING

EQUIPMENT: gas lamp, torches, matches
TIME NEEDED: 30+ mins

• A gas lamp is lit and placed in a small clearing in a wooded area. Four to six leaders (or older players) are armed with torches and locate themselves at least ten metres from the light. One blows a whistle to start the game and the players, who have been waiting back at base, must try to creep up and turn the lamp off without being spotted by the defenders.

• The defenders should not keep the torches on permanently, but switch them on and point them at any players they hear approaching, calling their name or description of their clothing. Spotted players must stand up and walk well away from the area before trying to attack again.

• When the lamp is extinguished, blow the whistle, send players back to base (checking the area for lazy players!), relight the lamp and blow the whistle for round two.

## FUGITIVE

EQUIPMENT: prepared 'Wanted' posters
TIME NEEDED: 45+ mins

• Before the game, which is best played in a built-up area, prepare 'Wanted' posters, featuring photographs of five (say) friends of yours. Players study the posters, which remain at base, and then set off to scour the defined playing area to look for the fugitives.

• They should note down (BUT NOT APPROACH) any fugitive they think they spot, indicating exactly where they were, what they were doing and what they were wearing. After 45 minutes, players return to base - which teams have spotted all five fugitives correctly?

# GOLDFINGER

EQUIPMENT: ten blocks of wood painted gold, two different coloured balls of wool

TIME NEEDED: 45+ mins

- Two teams set up a base at either end of a large playing area, in which their five gold bars, and a supervising leader, must be kept.

- Players have 'lives' attached to their upper arms (short lengths of wool, loosely tied. Alternatively, plastic straws held in the hand, or scarves tucked into a belt, can act as lives).

- On the starting whistle, players must try to raid the opposing team's base and steal a gold bar. If they get within three metres of the base untagged, they may take a gold bar and have safe passage back to their own base. Only a person with a 'life' intact may take a gold bar.

- If an attacker is tagged she must surrender her 'life' and must return to her own base in order to receive a new one and is out of the game until she does so.

- Defenders are not allowed within the 3m safety zone at their own base, unless receiving a new life or depositing an acquired gold bar.

- Winning team is that which is first to get all ten bars or which, at the end of the given time, has the most bars.

## SOUNDS FAMILIAR

EQUIPMENT: cards made up as detailed below, pens
TIME NEEDED: 30+ mins

• Teams (pairs or groups of three or four) are issued with a 'Sound Card'. This bears a numbered list of six or so noises, with a space alongside for a signature. Each team's list has the noises in a different order.

• Leaders are to hide themselves in the playing area (preferably dark woodland) and must occasionally and briefly make the sound allocated to them (ring a bell; sound a horn; go 'moo', grunt like a pig; blow a kazoo, play a radio...).

• Players are then set off and must visit the noise-makers in the order shown on their card, where they get the leader's signature.

• A leader will not sign if the box above his has not been signed, nor will he sign until all members of the team are present.

• Winning team is the first to complete their card.

## CONKERTHON

EQUIPMENT: lots of conkers (or sugar lumps)
TIME NEEDED: 20+ mins

• The conkers are scattered over the playing area and players, working as teams, must try to find them all.

• For every ten they find, they receive part of a rocket-launching equipment: a milk bottle, a small firework rocket, an empty matchbox, a safety match.

• Which team can find the conkers the quickest and be the first to fire a rocket to signal their achievement?

# STICKER PATROL

EQUIPMENT: sheets of small coloured sticky labels
TIME NEEDED: 45+ mins

• Four or five leaders take a sheet of stickers each - a different colour or shape for each leader - and disappear into the playing area (preferably dark woodland).

• Players are set off and must try to find the leaders. When they do so, they collect a sticker which they must take back to base and give to a 'Controller', who sticks it on the player's teams' space on a master chart. The controller will only accept one sticker per player at a time.

• Players having deposited stickers then try to find other leaders - they may visit any leaders as often as they like, but MUST return to base to deposit stickers before finding a leader.

• On the final whistle, players return to base to see which team has the most stickers. No stickers may be handed to the controller after the whistle has been blown. Points are allocated to each colour/shape, depending on how many have been distributed.

# MONKEY TAG

EQUIPMENT: none TIME NEEDED: 30+ mins

• This needs to be played in a heavily wooded area and is played in a similar way to normal 'Tag'.

• Two players are chosen to be 'It' and they must try to tag the others. Players are safe if they jump up and grab hold of a branch of a tree. They may not grab hold of the same branch twice running and, if caught, they become It as well and help catch the others. Catchers may not wait around until a player drops from a branch.

# KICK THE CAN

EQUIPMENT: an empty catering-size tin
TIME NEEDED: 45+ mins

• The tin is placed in the centre of a clearing in the woods and a player is chosen to be the Keeper.

• She closes her eyes and counts to 100 while the others go of and hide.

• The Keeper must then wander off and try to spot the players and make them her prisoner. She does this by shouting "I see Gavin in the pink t-shirt behind the wall" and returning to the can and tapping it with her foot.

• Gavin must then walk to the clearing and sit down at its edge as her prisoner.

• If, however, Gavin thinks that he can get to the can before the Keeper taps it, he should run for it and try to boot it out of the clearing.

• If he succeeds he is free (and so are any other prisoners) and must run off and hide before the Keeper has time to replace the tin and start spotting again.

• At any time, a player may try to surprise the Keeper and kick the can.

• If he succeeds, without getting identified and beaten to the can by the Keeper, he and any prisoners are freed.

• Vary the Keeper if prisoners keep getting freed.

# COMBAT

EQUIPMENT: one card per player (see below)

TIME NEEDED: 45+ mins

• Players divide into two teams and each make their way to a base (a tree or post) at opposite ends of the playing area. The playing area is divided in two - players are safe in their own half.

• Each player is issued a card which has been prepared in advance thus: General (10 points); Major (8 points); Captain (6 points); Sergeant (5 points); Corporal (4 points); Private (3 points) and Spy (1 point). There should always be two spies and one General, quantities of other ranks may vary.

• On the starting whistle, players must try to enter the opposing team's half and tag one of their players. They compare their two cards and the holder of the lowest card becomes prisoner of the other (matching cards represent a draw and both are free). The higher rank always wins except that a General is beaten by a spy.

• The prisoner must be escorted to the victor's base where she must stay with her hand touching the team's base tree. New prisoners hold hands with the others to form a chain.

• Prisoners may be freed by a fellow player managing to touch the prisoner on the end of the chain (ie: farthest from the base tree) without having been tagged by a member of the defending team.

## LETTERBOXING

EQUIPMENT: three 'letterboxes' (cardboard boxes will do), 'postcards' - see below - five times the number of players
TIME NEEDED: 45+ mins

- Three leaders take a postbox each (one labelled 'Scotland', one 'Wales' and one 'England') and hide in the woods.
- Players are divided into teams and all queue up at the 'Post Office', where they are given at random a postcard, on which is written either 'Scotland', 'Wales' or 'England'.
- Teams write their name on the back and then go to find the correct postbox and post their cards. When a player has posted a card, he returns to the post office to collect a new one.
- Leaders with the post boxes may move about freely.
- At the end of the given time, the boxes are opened and a point is awarded to teams for each card that has been correctly delivered (that is, a Wales card in the Wales box). Cards with no team name on the back do not count.

## STRINGAMBLE

EQUIPMENT: lots of short pieces of white string
TIME NEEDED: 45+ mins

- The pieces of string are scattered around a given area in some dark woods and are guarded by a team of five or six players armed with torches.
- Other players, in two teams, must try to creep up undetected and take pieces of the string. If spotted by the defenders, players must return to the edge of the playing area before attacking again. Any string retrieved is taken to a team's base where it is tied to other pieces.
- On the final whistle, teams discover which of their two teams has the longest pieces of assembled string.

# BATTLE

EQUIPMENT: small cards (see below) - ten times the number of players, three master lists

TIME NEEDED: 45+ mins

• Players form into teams and go with a leader (or team leader) to make a base at the edge of the playing area.

• The leader has a bag containing cards bearing pictures or names on them such as: Diamond Ring, Gold Bar, Carriage Clock, Gold Watch, Antique Vase. Each player is given ONE card.

• On the whistle, players run to the playing area and tag a member of an opposing team. The two then make their way to a leader wandering around the playing area who is holding a master list. This list contains all of the items in a specific order - the three leaders' lists are each in a different order.

• The two players show their cards and the leader checks her list. The player whose item is highest on her list wins and takes the loser's card.

• The loser returns to his base to get a new card, the winner returns to his base to deposit one of his cards before tagging someone else.

• NOTE: Players should only have one card at a time. If they have two when they get to a leader with another player, they must decide which card to use BEFORE seeing the other's card and, if they lose, they lose all cards they are carrying.

# CUSTOMS AND EXCISE

EQUIPMENT: quantities of two different types of 'contraband' (see below), wool for 'lives'

TIME NEEDED: 45+ mins

• Players form into two unequal teams, one fifth of the players become the Customs Officials, the rest are Smugglers.

• A playing area is defined in dark woodland with a base at each end and an imaginary line down the centre, as on a football pitch, which the Customs Officials are to patrol.

• At one base waits half of the smugglers and a large quantity of one type of item (such as empty film canisters), at the other base waits the rest of the smugglers and a second type of contraband (such as water containers or large bowls).

• Each smuggler has a woollen 'life' tied loosely around her upper arm.

• When the whistle blows, smugglers must try to take one piece of contraband at a time from their base to the other base, without getting spotted by the Customs Officials who are armed with torches.

• If a Customs Official spots a smuggler, she must surrender her 'life' and the contraband (if she was carrying any) and must return to her base for a new life.

• The game ends when all contraband has been exchanged between bases.

*A Pocketful of Programmes*

## THE NAME GAME

EQUIPMENT: none TIME NEEDED: 45+ mins

• Five or six leaders wander off into the wooded playing area and each is given a funny name, such as Dopey Desmond, Giggling Gertrude... and so on.

• Players are then set off to find a leader and ask him his name. The leader will say his name and then the name of another leader.

• Visiting players must then go off and find this new leader (no other leader will do) where they will be given the name of the next leader to be found.

• They should say which leader they have just visited to prove that they meant to visit a particular leader.

• Leaders always send players on to the same person, so that they will eventually complete a full circle, regardless of where they started.

## SIGN THIS

EQUIPMENT: pens and paper TIME NEEDED: 30+ mins

• Leaders and helpers (as many as possible) disappear into the wooded playing area and hide (but not too well!).

• Players are then set off with a piece of paper and must try to locate each leader and obtain their signatures. They should do this quietly in order that they do not let on to other players where the leaders are hiding, since the player with the most signatures at the end is the winner.

• Players should be told a silly password to say in order to get a signature and, to spin the game out, some leaders may only give a signature in return for a song, joke, gift (a stone, three different leaves and so on...)

# TARGET PRACTICE

EQUIPMENT: dried peas, five washing-up bowls
TIME NEEDED: 45+ mins

• A quarter of the players become the defenders and must guard lots of washing up bowls placed around a clearing in a dark, wooded area, armed with torches.

• The remaining players are attackers and are each issued with five dried peas by a leader at a base.

• On the starting whistle, the players must try to creep up and deposit as many dried peas as possible in the bowls without being spotted by the defenders.

• The defenders should not keep the torches on permanently, but switch them on and point them at any players they hear approaching, calling their name or giving a description of their clothing.

• Spotted players must stand up and walk well away from the area before trying attack again.

• Players should throw peas into the bowls - it's a great test of accuracy (and luck!) and quiet movements will not give away their positions to the defenders. More peas are obtainable (in quantities of five per visit) from the base.

• When the final whistle blows, if (say) 50 peas or more are in the bucket, the attackers have won, if not, the defenders have won.

*Pocketful of Programmes*

# ICE BREAKERS
## A collection of games and activities to help people get to know one another

## CIRCLE NAMES

EQUIPMENT: none

PLAYERS: eight or more  PLAYING TIME: 15+ mins

* Players sit in a circle and have a sticker on their chests, bearing their first names.

* The leader of the game begins a rhythm, which everyone follows, by slapping his thighs, clapping his hands then clicking first his left then his right fingers, giving a 'one, two, three four' rhythm.

* The leader starts off by saying HIS name on the first finger click, followed by ANOTHER player's name on the second click. That player must then, on the next first click, repeat her name and then choose someone else's name for the second click, looking at him as she does so.

* After ten minutes or so of this, remove all of the stickers and play again. Who can remember everyone's names?

## INTRODUCTIONS

EQUIPMENT: none
PLAYERS: any number    PLAYING TIME: 10+ mins

• Players wander slowly around the playing area for five minutes.

• Whenever they get eye contact with someone, they take it in turns to introduce each other.

• When the time is up, players sit in a circle and each is challenged to name each person around the circle in turn. Make this harder by adding that players must describe their job or hobby when they meet each other.

## WHO'S GOT THE BALL?

EQUIPMENT: a tennis ball or other small object
PLAYERS: ten or more    PLAYING TIME: 15+ mins

• Players sit in a tight circle, with their hands held behind them. One player stands in the centre of the circle and must close her eyes while the ball is given to a player in the circle to pass around.

• Players must pass the ball, without hanging on to it, around in a clockwise direction while the player in the middle (who by now has her eyes open!), must try to identify exactly where the ball has got to. At any time, she can call 'STOP' and she then has to say the name of the person who has the ball. Can she spot the ball's whereabouts and give the holder's correct name?

## CIRCLE CHUCK

EQUIPMENT: a football
PLAYERS: eight or more   PLAYING TIME: 10+ mins
- Players stand in a big circle and throw the ball to one another at random. When a player catches the ball she must say her name before throwing it to another player.
- Round two is similar, except a player must say the name of the person he is throwing the ball to as it is in mid-flight - how many people correctly remembered everybody's names?
- Round three further tests this. A player throws the ball to someone but, instead of saying the name of that person, she says "To Emma" (for example). The payer catching the ball must then throw it to Emma, whilst calling out a new name for Emma to throw the ball to .

## SKINNING THE SNAKE

EQUIPMENT: none
PLAYERS: five or more    PLAYING TIME: 15+ mins
- Players stand in a line, facing forward. They bend over and place their RIGHT arm through the legs of the person in front of them. They then pass their LEFT arm back through their own legs and grab the right hand of the person behind them.
- When they are all ready, the player at the back starts the snake-skinning process by crawling through the legs of all the players in front of him. The player who was next to him will follow him through the legs and so on, until the snake has been skinned and all players are standing in one long line.
- At no time must players let go of anyone's hands. Try running this as an inter-team speed challenge... alternatively, see how many people you can achieve this with (1993 record in Middlesex stands at 211).

## UNDER THE BLANKET

EQUIPMENT: a blanket
PLAYERS: eight or more   PLAYING TIME: 10+ mins
- Players sit in a large circle and one player leaves the room.
- One remaining player is chosen to sit in the centre of the circle and has a blanket placed over her.
- The first player re-enters and must try to identify the person under the blanket, either by a process of elimination with those who are left or by identifying the voice - the player under the blanket may only say 'Hello' to whatever the other player asks.
- This may be played with name badges on - although the one on the player under the blanket won't be visible.

## EXPERTS

EQUIPMENT: none
PLAYERS: any number    PLAYING TIME: 15+ mins
- A leader sits in one of two chairs arranged in front of the rest of the players and announces that she is the interviewer on a brand new chat show. She has got some interesting guests lined up and will proceed to interview them live.
- She then invites a player to sit with her and introduces him as 'Professor Dave Ludlow' (for example), describing his profession accordingly, such as: 'The world's foremost expert on beekeeping'.
- The interviewer then asks numerous questions of the 'guest' who must talk knowledgeably about his specialist subject. Questions should not be those requiring 'yes' or 'no' answers, in order to extract as much 'information' as possible. The interview's length depends on the player.

## DIZZY DAVE

EQUIPMENT: none
PLAYERS: eight or more  PLAYING TIME: 8+ mins

• Players sit in a circle and must introduce themselves by saying their first name, preceded by a description stating with the same letter as their name. For example: Dizzy Dave, Riotous Rebecca, Timid Timothy, Bright Benji, Poorly Pauline... and so on.

• Continue around the circle as many times as you can - players could lose a 'life' if they can't think of a description when it is their turn.

## WHO AM I ?

EQUIPMENT: lots of sticky labels
PLAYERS: any number  PLAYING TIME: 15+ mins

• Each player has a sticker placed on their back, on which is written the name of a famous person (fictional or real) or of a job description (dustman, politician etc).

• A player must try to identify the name written on her sticker. She does this by approaching another player who reads her sticker and then mimes what is written. When she has guessed correctly, she goes to the leader and swaps it for a new sticker.

• This is an excellent 'coming-in' game.

## SEALED ORDERS

EQUIPMENT: lots of 'sealed orders'
PLAYERS: any number    PLAYING TIME: 15+ mins

• A 'sealed order' is simply a task written on a piece of folded up paper. The leader gives each player a sealed order which must be accomplished as quickly as possible.

• Tasks could include: 'Find Richard White and introduce him to Jean Clowes'; 'Get the autograph of everyone whose second name contains the letter S'; 'Find out the names of everyone's pets'... and so on.

• Once a mission has been accomplished, players may be given a new sealed order. Continue until all have arrived or until the time is up.

## AUTOGRAPH HUNTING

EQUIPMENT: pens and prepared lists
PLAYERS: any number    PLAYING TIME: 15+ mins

• Players are given sheets of paper containing a list of 'qualities'. They must then find other players with those qualities and get them to sign their names in the given space on the sheet.

• Players my only sign for one quality on each sheet, in order to ensure that players talk to everybody.

• 'Qualities' could include: Someone who's left-handed, Someone with a watch. Someone with glasses. Someone with fair hair. Someone with a brother. Someone with a bicycle...

## LORD OF THE RING

EQUIPMENT: none

PLAYERS: eight or more   PLAYING TIME: 10+ mins

• Players sit in a large circle then (and this can be tricky, but it's good to watch!) they arrange themselves so that they are lying down with their head resting gently on another player's stomach. The end result should be a circle of players with their heads on one person's stomach and with someone else's head on theirs.

• A player starts by saying 'Ha Ha Ha!' The player with her head on player one's stomach must repeat this, followed by player three and so on.

• See how fast this can travel around the circle - and what's the betting that everybody breaks out into uncontrollable laughter as their heads are bounced around on chuckling tums!

## THE HUMAN KNOT

EQUIPMENT: none

PLAYERS: six or more   PLAYING TIME: 10+ mins

• Players stand in a circle with their arms outstretched in front of them.

• They grab the hands of two different players (and not their neighbours), one in each hand.

• Their mission is to unscramble the knot and end up in one large circle with their hands still linked.

## BABY GIGGLES

EQUIPMENT: photographs (see below), pens and paper
PLAYERS: six or more     PLAYING TIME: 20+ mins

• Before the meeting, course, holiday or party, participants have been asked to bring with them a picture of them taken when they were under three years old.

• These are pinned around the walls and numbered.

• Players are given a sheet of paper and must try to guess which baby was which player. They should write down the picture number alongside the player's name.

• This game means that players will have to approach each other and ask each other's names in order to complete the game.

## JUST A MINUTE

EQUIPMENT: none
PLAYERS: any number     PLAYING TIME: 10+ mins

• Players have one minute in which to introduce themselves by telling their entire life history.

• It is interesting to see what individuals think are the most important things that have happened in their lives.

# TREASURE HUNTS
## A selection of ideas for treasure hunts, designed for minimum leader involvement

*NOTE: Treasure hunts are many and varied but often follow the same pattern of finding a clue to lead to another. The following ideas offer alternatives which could be used as a basis for broadening your repertoire!*

## HUNT THE PEG

EQUIPMENT: pegs, cards, paper and pens
TIME NEEDED: 30+ mins

• Beforehand, a leader has prepared 15 (say) tent pegs, each of which has a small piece of card attached bearing a letter.

• The pegs are hammered into the ground over the playing area.

• Players are given a paper and pen and must write down the letter of each peg they find. In other words, they must find which 15 letters of the alphabet have been used.

• When they have found all of the letters, they should re-arrange them into a word or words. If they are correct they receive a piece of the 'treasure'.

• In order to prolong the game, it is an idea to hold one peg back for 20 minutes or so, and subtly bash it in when nobody is looking!

# COLOUR BLOCK

EQUIPMENT: cards, coloured pencils, prepared sheets (see below)

TIME NEEDED: 60 mins

• Beforehand, prepare 25 cards, lettered A to Y, each with a piece of string and a coloured pencil attached. These cards are then pinned up around as wide a playing area as you wish - don't forget to tell the players where the boundaries are.

• Also prepare a grid containing five rows and five columns, each box containing a letter.

• Players are given a copy of the grid each and must go to the playing area and find the lettered cards. When they find one, they use the pencil to colour in the appropriately numbered box on the grid.

• For every ROW of five boxes they complete (as in Bingo), they may return to base and be rewarded with a piece of treasure (a sweet). The leader marks a line through rows that have been claimed and players go off to try and find elusive letters to build up remaining rows.

• This game provides hours of fun and needs only one sitting-down leader to run it!

# GRIDLOCK

EQUIPMENT: see below
TIME NEEDED: 60 mins

- Beforehand, prepare a grid, similar to a Battleships board, with 26 columns and, say, 20 rows (enough to fit easily on a sheet of A4 paper). Label the grid A to Z across the top and 1 to 20 down the left-hand side. Players will each need a copy of this grid.
- On one copy of the grid, fill in some squares to form a few simple words which will spell out where the treasure is. Each letter needs a height of five squares, plus one above and below as a space. Words could be: IN THE VAN or SEE JOHN SMITH.
- Next, you will need to prepare a lot of cards bearing grid references (A7; X13 and so on). These grid references are those of each filled-in square that makes up letters on your master grid. These grid reference cards are then pinned up at random around the playing area.
- Players are given a copy of the blank grid and a pen and go off in search of grid reference cards. When they find one they colour in the box it refers to.
- Eventually, they will be able to make out letters, then complete words.
- You may wish to fill in some of the squares in advance - you will not need a card for any such squares.
- As soon as players can read the words they should go there to claim their share of the treasure.

## TELEPHONE TRAIL

EQUIPMENT: coins for the telephone, maps
TIME NEEDED: 60+ mins

• Teams are given a map of the local area and a handful of 10 and 20 pence pieces. Each team is told to make their way to a particular public telephone, from which they must make a call to a central number.

• The leader manning the central number will ask the team's name/number and the number of the box they are calling from. They will then be given the reference of the next telephone to visit, from where they repeat the process.

• A simple circuit can be devised whereby teams start and finish at a particular telephone before returning to the base - first team back gets first choice of the treasure.

## TRIG TRAIL

EQUIPMENT: local Ordnance Survey map
TIME NEEDED: 45 mins

• Teams can follow traditional treasure hunt clues, each of which leads to where the next clue is hidden. Also hidden at these points are one of six grid references labelled in pairs (ie: A & AA; B & BB, C & CC and D & DD).

• When a grid reference is found it is plotted on the map.

• When all references are found, a pencil line should be drawn to connect the pairs thus: A to AA; B to BB, C to CC

• The treasure will be buried (and why not actually bury it for a change?) somewhere in the small triangle between where the three lines intersect.

• The beauty of this is that all six grid references are needed before the location can be determined.

# ACTIVITIES
## A selection of activities to challenge and inspire young and old

### SIGNALLING

EQUIPMENT: per team: a torch battery, bulb, wires, sticks
TIME NEEDED: 20+ mins
• Using the materials provided, build a device to send morse code messages to a team sited some distance away.

### BLINDFOLD CATERING

EQUIPMENT: blindfolds, icing sugar, eggs, peppermint essence, food colouring
TIME NEEDED: 15+ mins
• Each person must be blindfolded and must use their sense of touch to make peppermint creams using the ingredients provided.

### EGG DROPPING

EQUIPMENT: per team: a raw egg, a sheet of newspaper, 1m of adhesive tape, three balloons
TIME NEEDED: 15+ mins
• Teams must invent some way of keeping the egg unbroken when it is thrown high into the air by a leader. (It can be done easily by sandwiching the egg between two partly-inflated balloons, taped together - but don't tell them until they've tried it!)

# GOING TO CAMP

EQUIPMENT: one conker/stone per team, lots of home-made '£20' notes, pictures of camping equipment cut from catalogues
TIME NEEDED: 30 mins

• Each team is trying to raise enough money to go away to camp and must buy the following:

    - one tent (£300)
    - one set of cooking equipment (£20)
    - six sleeping bags (£20 each)
    - one box of food (£20)

• To raise the money, player one in each team runs to a leader and holds both hands in front, one of which must contain the conker/stone. The leader will try to guess in which hand the player is holding the stone.

• If the leader is correct, the player returns to her team and gives the conker to player two for his turn. If the leader does not find the conker, he must give the player '£20' which is then taken back to add to the team's funds. Player two then takes the conker for his turn... and so on.

• Another leader should act as shopkeeper to sell the pictures of the equipment - and to 'fine' teams whose members are wandering around out of turn! Which team can achieve their target first?

## WOOD, COTTON, PLASTIC

EQUIPMENT: paper and pens        TIME NEEDED: 15 mins
• Participants are given a piece of paper and a pen and must wander around the playing area and write down everything they can find made from wood, cotton or plastic. Compare lists at the end and award points to participants who spotted things that nobody else did.

## 3-D PICTURES

EQUIPMENT: scissors, wrapping paper, self-adhesive foam pads (eg: mirror tile fixers)
TIME NEEDED: 30 mins
• Using wrapping paper with busy, colourful scenes on them, participants cut out lots of the pictures.
• Using the sticky pads, they stick individual pictures on top of the original picture on a flat sheet of the paper. Build this up by using another pad and a smaller cut out detail from the picture to provide a three-dimensional picture.
• It may sound complicated, but do try it and you'll be surprised with the results.

## HAVE WE GOT NEWS FOR YOU!

EQUIPMENT: lots of fairly recent newspapers, scissors, felt-tipped pens

TIME NEEDED: 20+ mins

• Working individually or in teams, participants look through the newspapers and cut out about 10 to 20 headlines.

• They should then cut out or blacken one or more words in the headline.

• When everybody is ready, participants take it in turns to guess the missing words in other people's headlines, gaining a point for each correct (or nearly correct) answer.


## ALPHABETTI-GETTI

EQUIPMENT: none

TIME NEEDED: 30 mins

• A simple scavenger hunt which will enable participants to explore an area, the boundaries of which you have described in advance.

• Participants have 30 minutes in which to find 26 objects - one for each letter of the alphabet. For example: A = acorn; B = book; C = crayon; D = dust...


## NOISEMAKER - 1

EQUIPMENT: thin plastic drinking straws, scissors

TIME NEEDED: 10 mins

• Cut the straw to a length of about 8 to 10cm and flatten one end, using your teeth or the handle of the scissors.

• Using two snips, cut the flattened end into a point. Place this end into your mouth and blow - it should produce an ear-piercing screech. Experiment with different lengths.

*Pocketful of Programmes*

## NOISEMAKER - 2

EQUIPMENT: paper
TIME NEEDED: 5+ mins

• Tear a strip of paper roughly 15cm x 4cm and fold it in half (to become 7.5 x 4cm).

• In the centre of the folded edge, make a short (1cm long) tear at right angles to the fold. Hold the folded paper between index and middle finger, with the fold and tear pointing away from you (on the knuckle side of your hand). Fold the two sides of paper that are closest to you apart and hold to your mouth. Blow hard into the paper and listen to the screech!

## CASTLE BUILDING

EQUIPMENT: lots of sheets of newspaper, bamboo canes, adhesive tape.
TIME NEEDED: 30+ mins

• The canes should be stuck firmly into the ground to form a square, with sides roughly 2-3m in length. A castle may then be constructed, using paper for the walls, secured with adhesive tape (or a stapler). (If you have a local magazine printer, ask them for the end of a roll of paper.)

• Once built, and decorated if you wish, you could hold a battle, with participants wearing home-made helmets, shields and tabards, perhaps.

• Provide about 30 newspaper balls per castle and, on the word 'GO', teams have to throw these into other castles. At the end of the given time, the castle with the least cannonballs in it is the winner.

• For a frenetic finale, cannonballs could be squares of kitchen towel (or sponges) soaked in bowls of water - whichever castle is still standing when the whistle blows is the winner!

## MINI FIRST AID KIT

EQUIPMENT: per person: empty film canister, antiseptic wipe, paper tissue, two sticking plasters, white label
TIME NEEDED: 15+ mins

• A useful little kit for young people exploring woods who are likely to scratch themselves! They should squeeze the above items in the canister and apply a white label on the outside, onto which they should draw a white cross on a green background (the first aid sign) and their name. Be sure to brief them as to how to use the contents and remind youngsters to seek adult help for big cuts.

## TELEVISION BINGO

EQUIPMENT: card, pens
TIME NEEDED: 20+ mins

• Mark out a grid on a piece of card, to give about seven columns and five rows.

• Blank out eight of the boxes using a pen. In the other boxes, draw pictures of everyday objects, such as a kettle, post box, dog, tree, cloud, vicar... and so on.

• Participants should prepare a few of these cards, all using the same objects but putting them in different positions on the cards.

• Turn the television on and, whenever an item on a card is seen on the screen, it may be covered with a piece of paper or ticked with a pencil.

• Winner is the first person to complete a horizontal line. Then you can play for a vertical line or even a full house.

## ICE CUBE IDEAS

EQUIPMENT: ice cubes
TIME NEEDED: 30+ mins
• Each participant is given an ice cube and the winner is the first to melt it completely, without using external heat sources.
• Next, play a game of indoor ice hockey, using large ice blocks as the pucks and rolled-up newspaper for sticks and with two players at a time trying to score a goal.
• Then, see who can build an igloo using ice cubes.
• Lastly, hold a 'paperchase' where two participants run off and deposit ice cubes along their route. Following participants are set off ten minutes later and will have to hurry to follow the trail before it melts away!

## BIODEGRADING LAB

EQUIPMENT: plastic tub, soil, paper, card & plastic strips.
TIME NEEDED: 25+ mins (plus long-term observation)
• Fill a plant pot or empty ice cream tub with ordinary garden soil (not potting compost).
• Into this, bury 10cm lengths of cardboard, paper, polystyrene, plastic, rice paper and paper tissue so that they stick out a few centimetres at the top.
• Keep the soil damp (leave it outside if possible) and check the strips every few days to see which material biodegrades the most quickly.
• This activity could provide a useful stimulus for environmental/recycling-related projects.

# MONSTER BUBBLES

EQUIPMENT: metal coat hanger, bowl, washing-up liquid, corn syrup

TIME NEEDED: 15+ mins

• Mix up three cupfuls of water, one cup of washing-up liquid and half a cup of corn syrup and you'll have a super-strong bubble mix. This mix works best if made three or four hours before you plan to use it.

• Using fuse wire, metal coat hangers or pipecleaners, make as large a circle as you wish, securing the ends to form a sturdy handle.

• Dip the circle in the liquid and, with a deft movement of the hand through the air, a huge bubble will form. Don't try this indoors or on someone's prize lawn - concrete or paving stones are best.

• Have a contest to see who can blow the biggest bubble or who can keep their airborne the longest by blowing or fanning it. What about bubble basketball?

# A BRIDGE TOO FAR

EQUIPMENT: wooden lolly sticks, cotton, elastic bands

TIME NEEDED: 30+ mins

• Using the equipment provided, build a sturdy bridge from lolly sticks (available in bulk from craft shops). The bridge should be self-supporting and should span a 3m wide chasm.

• Older participants will not need rubber bands or cotton to lash the joints, whereas younger participants might.

## EGG RACING

EQUIPMENT: scissors, glue, adhesive tape, a hard-boiled egg, elastic bands, strips of card, wood and any other junk that's lying around.

TIME NEEDED: 45+ mins

• Teams have to construct a vehicle which will be able to transport the egg (suitably decorated) along a flat course under its own power.

• See which team's contraption is the best with regards to distance travelled, speed and general appeal of design.

## BUTTER MAKING

EQUIPMENT: some fresh full-cream milk, a jam jar with a screw-on lid

TIME NEEDED: 25+ mins

• Participant quarter-fill the jam jar with milk, screw the lid on and shake it in order to produce butter.

• This will be done more quickly if an automatic shaker can be invented - possibly using a stationary bicycle?

• Who can produce enough butter to spread on some bread first?

## ACCURATE DRAWING

EQUIPMENT: pens and paper

TIME NEEDED: 10+ mins

• Participants are read out a list of items which they must attempt to draw at their actual size - playing card, matchbox, ballpoint pen, paperback book...

• Award points not for artistic skills but for the accuracy of their measurements.

## AUTOMATIC CATCHER

EQUIPMENT: bamboo canes, elastic bands, string...
TIME NEEDED: 30+ mins

• Participants are requested to design a gadget capable of firing a tennis ball vertically into the air - and then catching it again. Obviously, to be able to catch it again, the gadget must fire the ball absolutely vertically.

## NIGHT LIGHTS

EQUIPMENT: candlewax, empty food tin, corrugated cardboard, sturdy sticks, fuse wire
TIME NEEDED: 15+ mins

• Teams use the given equipment to produce a nightlight capable of burning safely out-of doors for several hours.

## PIPELINES

EQUIPMENT: lots of plastic straws
TIME NEEDED: 30+ mins

• Participants work in pairs or small teams to construct the longest continuous pipeline possible, using only straws (no tape allowed). Test how watertight they are by dripping (or blowing) water through them in turn.

## HAMMOCK BUILDING

EQUIPMENT: a blanket/groundsheet, sisal string/nylon cord)
TIME NEEDED: 25+ mins

• Participants are to design and build a sturdy hammock, capable of holding the weight of one of the participants.

• A simple way would be to tie an overhand knot at each corner of the blanket, then tie one end of a length of string to a knot using a sheet bend or similar strong knot. The four lengths of string can now be secured to conveniently-sited trees or guyed poles.

## MASTERCHEF

EQUIPMENT: a selection of foods: cereals, chocolate, dried fruit, treacle, condensed milk, icing sugar...
TIME NEEDED: 30+ mins

• Participants are given access to a pile of bits and pieces, which could include items listed above. They should then attempt to create a tasty dish, presented in as attractive a way as possible.

• Award points for appearance and for taste.

## EGG-A-THON

EQUIPMENT: one raw egg per team
TIME NEEDED: at least four minutes!

• At the start of an activity, weekly meeting or day's event, issue each team with a raw egg (marked by the leader). Ask them to present it, hardboiled, at the end of the activity. Boiling the egg must not get in the way of completing the main activity and no leader should be aware that it is being done - if so, points may be deducted.

# MOUSETRAP HEIST

EQUIPMENT: per team - one mousetrap, bamboo canes, string, paper clips...

TIME NEEDED: 30+ mins

• A mousetrap is armed and placed on an upended brick. Six metres away is a line, behind which stand the team and the rest of the equipment.

• Their mission is to retrieve the mousetrap without it going off. They are not allowed to cross the line but have to do everything by remote control.

• The leaders will be on hand to reset mousetraps and to count how many failed attempts each team has before succeeding.

# WITNESS

EQUIPMENT: a cash box

TIME NEEDED: 15+ mins

• During a busy part of a weekly meeting, a camp or any other such activity, a person enters and calmly picks something up and leaves. Leaders should ignore the visitor.

• Ten minutes later, a leader should discover that something has been taken - participants are required to draw an 'identikit' picture of the thief, noting down height, approximate weight, distinguishing features and so on.

• When all have finished, the 'thief' (a friend of yours who is unknown to the participants) enters and their descriptions are checked for accuracy.

## BOOMERANG MAKING

EQUIPMENT: Stiff card, scissors or craft knives
TIME NEEDED: 25+ mins

• Participants are challenged to make mini boomerangs which can be thrown or flicked from a table edge. Are traditional boomerang shapes the best or can they invent shapes which fly for longer or which return more often?

## MAKE A JOKE BOOK

EQUIPMENT: paper, pens
TIME NEEDED: 30+ mins

• Most young people enjoy telling jokes, so why not get them to write down their favourites in one place?

• Participants are given plenty of sheets of A4 paper, folded in half to give them four A5-sized sides to write jokes on and draw cartoons. Slot all completed pages together to give a unique booklet of your group's favourite gags.

• If undertaken as a longer-term project, the pages could be copied and the booklet sold to raise money for charity or for your group funds.

## PAPER FOLDING

EQUIPMENT: lots of different types of paper
TIME NEEDED: 5+ mins

• A quick 'filler' activity which could keep participants occupied for hours!

• All they have to do is try and fold a sheet of paper in half, then in half again, and again - a total of EIGHT times. It's virtually impossible, but get them to experiment with tissue, and huge sheets of newspaper and see how they fare.

# HIGHWAY CODE SURVEY

EQUIPMENT: current copies of the Highway Code
TIME NEEDED: 30+ mins

• Teams should go for a walk around their local area, armed with a copy of the Highway Code. They should then note down any examples of the Code being broken.

• They share their findings with other teams and see if there are any parts of the Code which are broken more frequently than others. This could lead into a road safety project.

# PET ROCKS

EQUIPMENT: lots of pebbles, paint
TIME NEEDED: 20+ mins

• In the 1970s, people paid a lot of money in shops for 'Pet Rocks' - pebbles with interesting shapes and which had faces painted on them or, in some instances, simply had those small black and white plastic 'joggle' eyes glued on them. These were the ideal pets as they needed no feeding or taking for walks and didn't bite.

• Participants could find their own interestingly shaped pebbles and turn them into their own 'pet rocks'. Varnishing the finished beastie will enhance its appearance.

# PAPER AEROPLANE-A-THON

EQUIPMENT: paper TIME NEEDED: 20+ mins

• Hold a paper aeroplane-building competition. Allow teams or individuals to practice for a while and then to present three different paper aeroplanes each to enter into three separate competitions: Longest distance covered; Best acrobatics; Accuracy.

54

# INCIDENT HIKE BASES
## A collection of activities ideal for use as bases in incident hikes or which may be used as general activities at any time

*NOTE: As a rule, manned bases, when completed, usually reward successful completion of an activity with either the next bit of the route or with a clue or a piece of treasure needed for the hike's theme.*

## SILENCE IS GOLDEN

EQUIPMENT: none
TIME NEEDED: 10 mins  TYPE: Manned

• The leader is sitting on the opposite side of a river to the approaching team. She can not speak and is unable to hear - the participants will soon discover this.

• The participants must communicate, using sign language or written messages, that they need the clue or instructions and must interpret the signed instructions from the leader which indicate where it is to be found.

## RADIOACTIVITY

EQUIPMENT: see below
TIME NEEDED: 10 mins  TYPE: Manned

• The clue is placed in the centre of a roped-off area, measuring about six metres in diameter.

• Teams have to retrieve the clue using whatever they can find, without entering the area. A supply of short garden canes, elastic bands and string may be provided

## MORSE INSPECTOR

EQUIPMENT: morse code light
TIME NEEDED: 12 mins  TYPE: Manned

• A battery-powered light is mounted in a tree, and is operated by wire by a leader who is sited some distance away.

• At the previous base, teams will have collected a copy of Morse code and will be on the lookout for the light.

• The leader slowly transmits the clue to the team three times, to give them a fair chance of translating it.

## CHANGING

EQUIPMENT: a car
TIME NEEDED: 15 mins  TYPE: Manned

• A stranded motorist needs a wheel changed on his car and doesn't know how. Participants must do it for him before proceeding. If they do it incorrectly, the motorist shows them how to do it properly, thus wasting the team several precious minutes.

## TREETOP TROUBLE

EQUIPMENT: see below
TIME NEEDED: 10 mins  TYPE: Manned

• A lady is stranded up a tree and has apparently broken her arm or leg (depending on the skills of the teams!).

• Teams must gently rescue her from the tree and provide first aid.

• Ropes and ladders are supplied nearby.

## BLINDFOLD TRAIL

EQUIPMENT: blindfolds, string
TIME NEEDED: 15 mins  TYPE: Manned
• The leader has prepared a lengthy trail through bushes and, when a team arrives, participants are blindfolded and must follow the trail to take them to the next checkpoint to continue their hike.

## CAR TROUBLE

EQUIPMENT: a car
TIME NEEDED: 45 mins  TYPE: Manned
• A motorist's car has broken down and needs a push start. Participants must push the car to enable the leader, whose car it is, to start it.  When successful, they receive their clue.
• Note: the driver can, of course, apply brakes and make it very hard for them start, in order to test players' stamina!

## SPIDER'S WEB

EQUIPMENT: ball of string, metal cutlery
TIME NEEDED: 15 mins  TYPE: Manned
• A web of string is set up between two trees, from which pairs of metal items, such as spoons, are hanging.
• Participants must try to get through the web without causing the cutlery to jangle together.
• If no trees, make a horizontal web using sticks knocked into the ground.

## STOP THIEF

EQUIPMENT: see below
TIME NEEDED: 12 mins  TYPE: Manned

• As the Team approaches, a mysterious person is jogging towards them, grunting and looking agitated, and who then gets into a car and drives off behind them.  The Team immediately comes upon a woman (a leader) who is distressed and claims that her handbag has been stolen.

• Participants are to compile an accurate description of the suspected assailant, and of the car.  They may then proceed.

## LOST AND FOUND

EQUIPMENT: costume jewellery
TIME NEEDED: 10 mins  TYPE: Manned

• A couple have accidentally lost a few items of jewellery in a given area.

• Participants have to locate each item before being allowed to proceed.

## GATE HOPPING

EQUIPMENT: sticks, string
TIME NEEDED: 10 mins  TYPE: Manned

• The team comes across a gate which is, apparently, electrified with 30 million volts.

• They must get each member of the team over it without anybody touching any part of the gate or its surrounds.

• Certain items may be made available if teams think using them will be of any use.

## MESSAGE IN A BOTTLE

EQUIPMENT: message, bottle, a lake, string
TIME NEEDED: 10 mins  TYPE: Manned

• A bottle contains the clue or next part of the route and is anchored four or five metres away from the bank in a lake or river.

• Teams are not permitted to enter the water but must retrieve the message. Vaguely useful items such as string and sticks may be left lying around for them to use.

## SELF DESTRUCT

EQUIPMENT: tape recorder
TIME NEEDED: 5 mins  TYPE: Manned

• Record the clue or directions to the next checkpoint on a cassette and place it in a tape recorder on the team's route, with the leader observing from a short distance away.

• Draw a big sign saying 'Do not play this cassette under any circumstances' - teams are guaranteed to play it! (If they don't, the leader should appear and let them do so.)

## JIGSAW

EQUIPMENT: a junior jigsaw
TIME NEEDED: 12 mins  TYPE: Manned

• Get an old junior jigsaw, the sort with under 20 pieces, and assemble it upside-down. Write the clue or directions on the reverse and break the jigsaw up again.

• Scatter the pieces in a given area and let the participants find the pieces, assemble the puzzle and get their next clue.

## GOOD EYESIGHT

EQUIPMENT: see below
TIME NEEDED: 5 mins   TYPE: Unmanned

• Teams have been directed to a particular tree. At eye level on this tree is pinned a notice saying that the next clue can be seen if they look above them (and that they are not to climb the tree).

• Written clearly in large, bold letters on a piece of board is the next clue. The board has been hoisted in place by a leader with a ladder.

• This base tests the participants' eyesight.

## HEAD THIS WAY

EQUIPMENT: a coloured lamp, flashing if possible
TIME NEEDED: not applicable   TYPE: Manned

• Teams have been directed to a specific location and told to look around them for a flashing coloured light. This should be sited half a mile or so away.

• Participants have no indication of where on the map it is but must try and make their way cross-country until they reach it and obtain the next clue.

## PHOTO-ROUTE

EQUIPMENT: copies of photographs
TIME NEEDED: not applicable   TYPE: unmanned

• Teams visit a checkpoint and collect an envelope (or open one given to them at the start, when they reach the given point). The envelope contains a series of photographs. Participants follow the route, as depicted in the pictures which were taken along the way. This leads them to the next checkpoint and the rest of their route details.

## THE BRAIN DRAIN

EQUIPMENT: drainpipe, film canister, water
TIME NEEDED: 10 mins  TYPE: manned

•  Lash or otherwise affix a two-metre length of drainpipe, firmly stoppered at the bottom end, to a tree or post. Place the clue inside a sealed plastic film canister and drop it into the pipe. Put a sign by the pipe saying where the clue is and provide useless things like string, elastic bands and paper clips and see if they can retrieve the clue.

•  What they really need is enough water (in a container hidden nearby, or in a stream) to simply float the clue to the top.

## THE KEY TO SUCCESS

EQUIPMENT: See below
TIME NEEDED: 12 mins  TYPE: manned

•  Borrow one of those key boxes you see at fetes, which have a locked door and 50 keys, only one opens the door.

•  The clue is placed in the box and the keys scattered in the immediate vicinity of the box.

•  Participants must find the right key in order to obtain their clue.

## LIGHTLINES

EQUIPMENT: two battery-powered lamps
TIME NEEDED: 6 mins  TYPE: unmanned

•  Lamps are hoisted into two trees and teams are told that the clue is pinned to a third tree in a direct line, 100 (say) paces away from one of the lit trees. They only need try two directions before finding the clue.

## WHISTLER

EQUIPMENT: a 'whistling keyring'
TIME NEEDED: 10 mins  TYPE: manned

• Obtain one of those cheap key rings which, when you whistle in its vicinity, emits a beeping noise.

• Attach this to the clue and hide it in a given area.

• Teams are told how to locate the clue by whistling around the area.

## SAFEBREAKERS

EQUIPMENT: a box, secured by 2 combination padlocks
TIME NEEDED: 10 mins  TYPE: Manned

• The clue is placed in the hinged box, which is locked using two hasps and two combination padlocks. We will assume that each padlock needs three numbers in order to open it.

• At the previous base, teams were each given a set of six general knowledge questions, the answers to each question forming one number of the required six. They should not appear in the correct order, although questions A, B and C should relate to padlock 1, and questions D, E and F to padlock 2.

• Upon arrival at this base, they should use trial and error to open the padlocks and retrieve the clue.

• Questions could be like these: How many wives did Henry XIII have? How many countries' flags make up the Union Flag?

# NOTES

# NOTES